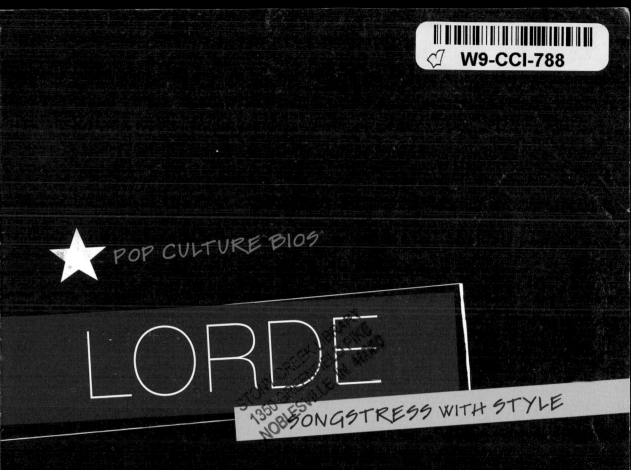

POP CULTURE BIOS

LORDE

SONGSTRESS WITH STYLE

HEATHER E. SCHWARTZ

Lerner Publications Company
MINNEAPOLIS

Lerner Publications Company
A division of Lerner Publishing Group, Inc.
241 First Avenue North
Minneapolis, MN 55401 USA

For reading levels and more information, look up this title at
www.lernerbooks.com.

Library of Congress Cataloging-in-Publication Data

Schwartz, Heather E.
    Lorde : songstress with style / by Heather E. Schwartz.
      pages   cm. — (Pop culture bios)
    Includes index.
    ISBN 978-1-4677-5717-1 (lib. bdg. : alk. paper)
    ISBN 978-1-4677-6100-0 (pbk.)
    ISBN 978-1-4677-6324-0 (EB pdf)
    1. Lorde, 1996– 2. Singers—New Zealand—Biography—
Juvenile literature. I. Title.
  ML3930.L67S34 2015
  782.42164092—dc23 [B]   2014023713

Manufactured in the United States of America
1 – PC – 12/31/14

Lorde performs at Coachella, a music festival held in Indio, California, in 2014.

INTRODUCTION

Lorde poses for a pic with Taylor Swift (RIGHT) at the 56th annual Grammy Awards.

It was January 26, 2014—the night of the 56th Grammy Awards. Nominated for four different awards, Lorde was all set to perform. There was just one problem. She was more than a little freaked out. In fact, she was so nervous that she almost felt sick. What if people didn't like her performance? What if they just didn't get it?

But when she stepped onstage, her talent took over. The music for "Royals" started up. Lorde lifted the microphone to her mouth. She began singing, her voice strong and confident. She was completely in control—of her sound, her movement, and the captivated crowd.

Lorde wowed the crowd with her impressive stage performance at the 2014 Grammies.

When "Royals" won Song of the Year, it beat major competition: songs by Pink, Katy Perry, Bruno Mars, and Macklemore & Ryan Lewis. Lorde also beat artists such as Sara Bareilles and Justin Timberlake when she won Best Pop Solo Performance.

She looked stunned and almost tearful as she gave her acceptance speech. **"This is the one thing that I did not expect…tonight, so thank you so much,"** she said.

Katy Perry also performed at the 56th Grammy Awards.

Lorde proudly shows off her two Grammy Awards.

Overwhelmed, she hurried offstage. Just a year after her first pro performance, Lorde was leaving the Grammys with two of the music industry's biggest awards.

Lorde takes a stroll with her dog in Los Angeles, California.

CHAPTER ONE

WORDS AT WORK

Lorde was born in Takapuna, New Zealand.

When Lorde was born, she wasn't Lorde at all. She was Ella Marija Lani Yelich-O'Connor. Growing up in New Zealand, she stood out from her family—but not because she was a scene-stealer. Compared to her younger sister, India; younger brother, Angelo; and older sister, Jerry, Lorde was considered quiet.

Lorde spent much of her time reading. Her mother, a poet, gave her lots of books. Her mother suggested authors such as Raymond Carver and Kurt Vonnegut. She recommended poetry too, but Lorde wasn't interested.

Lorde with her mom, Sonja

At school, Lorde's love of words brought her success. In 2007, she won a speech competition. Two years later, she and her classmates won second place in a worldwide literature quiz.

All this reading gave Lorde ideas and plenty of things to say. Drama classes helped her learn to make her opinions heard. And as she grew up, she discovered another way to let her thoughts and feelings out. She wrote short stories.

WELL-READ ROCKER

Lorde's favorite books include *What We Talk about When We Talk about Love* by Raymond Carver; *The Night in Question* by Tobias Wolff; *Everything Ravaged, Everything Burned* by Wells Tower; and *Battleborn* by Claire Vaye Watkins.

Claire Vaye Watkins, one of Lorde's favorite authors

Lorde was born on November 7, 1996.

Lorde Turns Lyrical

Around the age of twelve, Lorde's writing took a new turn. She started writing song lyrics. She wrote about her own life experiences. She also started singing in front of people. She joined a band called Extreme with six other students at her school. She started performing with her friend Louis McDonald too.

When Lorde and Louis played in a school competition, the twosome rocked the house. Louis's father recorded the performance. He even sent it to a talent scout.

Lorde at age 12 (2009) with her school band + interview at 7:58

Twelve-year-old Lorde (FAR LEFT) performs with the band Extreme.

1:52 / 6:52

Turning Pro

A tape of Lorde and Louis performing "Warwick Avenue" by Duffy wound up with Scott Maclachlan, head of talent recruitment at Universal Records in New Zealand. He liked what he saw and heard. But it wasn't the duo he wanted to sign. It was Lorde. He was impressed by her soulful voice. He thought she could become a professional singer.

At first, Lorde wasn't sure that was what she wanted. But at the age of thirteen, she signed a development deal with Universal Records. As a part of the deal, Lorde agreed to take voice lessons twice each week. She loved learning to improve her tone, which she thought was too nasally. As a bonus, she also got free tickets to concerts.

ONLY ORIGINALS

Universal Records initially wanted to put out an album of Lorde singing covers, or songs that others had already recorded. The plan was scrapped when she insisted on writing her own music.

Practice Makes Perfect

The deal also had a downside. Lorde was paired up with experienced songwriters to write new songs. But she felt as if they wanted to take over the process. She didn't get the chance to really contribute. And she didn't want to perform songs someone else wrote for her. She wanted to sing her own songs.

Finally, she met Joel Little, a songwriter with a background of performing in pop-punk bands. It was a perfect match. Lorde wrote ideas for lyrics on her computer and brought them to the studio. Joel helped her turn them into real lyrics that would work when set to music. In just one week, the pair wrote three songs, including "Royals."

Lorde and Joel Little accept the award for Song of the Year for "Royals" at the 2014 Grammy Awards.

CHAPTER TWO

FAST TRACK TO FAME

Lorde performs at Coachella in 2014.

Once she started writing lyrics, Lorde couldn't stop. No matter where she was, if she had an idea she'd write it down. She liked focusing on subjects other teenagers could relate to. She wrote about living in the suburbs and hanging out with friends.

After Lorde wrote more songs she liked, Universal Records was ready to release *The Love Club EP*. But Universal knew that Lorde was different. They wanted to release her music in a different way too.

Lorde attends a press conference in Mexico promoting her debut album, *Pure Heroine*.

Instead of putting her music on iTunes, Universal posted Lorde's songs for free on SoundCloud. Universal knew that if people listened to her music, her fan base would expand. Then more people would be willing to pay for her music later. The plan to create buzz around Lorde worked. Soon her song "Royals" went viral.

Not long after, Universal released Lorde's debut album, *Pure Heroine*. It included the songs "Royals," "Team," and "Tennis Court."

Public Praise

Meanwhile, Lorde started performing her music live. Her first audiences were mainly family and friends.

STRONG ONSTAGE

Lorde favors pants and solid, chunky shoes onstage. They're easy to move in and give her a sense of control. She also likes long dresses that make her feel feminine.

As she continued performing, her fame grew. Fans asked for autographs. The media praised her poise onstage. Musicians such as David Bowie, Elton John, and Selena Gomez tweeted and talked about her. They let the world know they admired Lorde's style.

Preserving Privacy

Lorde loved hearing her music on the radio. And she was psyched when "Royals" hit the No. 1 spot on *Billboard*'s Hot 100 chart in October 2013. The Hot 100 chart lists the most popular songs in the United States, and Lorde's song was at the top. It was great to be noticed and appreciated.

STYLE STARS

Lorde looks to David Bowie and Grace Jones for style inspiration.

PAPARAZZI =
photographers who take
pictures of celebrities

But fame had a strange side too. Lorde had to be on guard. Paparazzi followed her. And sometimes she was suspicious when asked to autograph pictures of herself. She could tell when someone didn't care about her music and just wanted to sell her autograph online.

She also learned that when she spoke, people paid *a lot* of attention. For example, when she publicly admired Kanye West and declared herself a feminist, the media spread her words quickly.

She had to give interviews. But she tried not to give too much away. Lorde wanted to stay mysterious.

"MINOR" MUSICIANS

Other singers have hit No. 1 on the *Billboard* Hot 100 chart before the age of eighteen too. They include Michael Jackson, Britney Spears, and Stevie Wonder.

CHAPTER THREE

CENTERED SUPERSTAR

Lorde performs at the Lollapalooza Argentina festival in 2014.

At the end of 2013, Lorde announced her first North American tour. She was also nominated for four Grammy Awards. She was low-key on Twitter, keeping her response to one word: "FOUR." But when the media asked for her reaction, she had more to say about how she felt.

"It's so prestigious. Everyone in the industry pays attention to this award and it's just the highest honor," she said. **"I couldn't be more grateful."**

Lorde greets excited fans.

Even before she won Song of the Year and Best Pop Solo Performance for "Royals," Lorde's North American tour was sold out.

COVER ME

In March 2014, music legend Bruce Springsteen covered Lorde's "Royals" at a show in New Zealand. When she heard about it, Lorde teared up.

A New Role

Over time, Lorde decided to open up in interviews. She didn't see the need to hide who she was. Instead, she wanted to be a role model for other young girls.

She spoke about feminism. She tweeted about her struggle with acne. She shared pictures of her makeup-free face. Lorde wanted to show her fans that her success came from being true to herself.

MOVING PERFORMANCE

Unlike many other performers, Lorde doesn't play an instrument while onstage. She says she'd rather just sing and move to her music.

Future Focus

In June 2014, Lorde announced more North American tour dates for the fall. With fans clamoring to see her perform, she is at the top of her career. But at seventeen years old, she isn't ready to say she's peaked just yet.

ON HER OWN

In 2014, Lorde had the chance to perform as an opening act on singer Katy Perry's world tour. She turned it down to focus on her own work and headline her own shows instead.

Katy Perry (LEFT) performs in Glasgow, Scotland, in 2014.

During her short rise to fame, Lorde has talked about her dreams for the future. She's said she wants to write music for other artists, such as Rihanna. She may also want to write more short fiction. She's writing songs for her second album too.

Lorde performs with Joan Jett (LEFT) and Dave Grohl (BACK) at the 29th annual Rock and Roll Hall of Fame concert.

While Lorde found success early in life, she also started working toward it early. She's not finished showing the world what she can do.

MAKING MAKEUP

Lorde loves lipstick. In spring 2014, Lorde teamed up with MAC cosmetics to design a lipstick and eyeliner collection for her fans.

LORDE
PICS!

Lorde performs at the 2014 Billboard Music Awards.

Lorde poses with the Brit Award she won in 2014.

SOURCE NOTES

6   "Lorde Wins Best Pop Solo Performance," YouTube video, 2:04, from the 54th Grammy Awards televised by CBS on January 26, 2014, posted by "The GRAMMYs," January 26, 2014, https://www.youtube.com/watch?v=hXm-3DJTGZw.

21 "FOUR," Twitter, posted by "@lordemusic," December 7, 2013, https://twitter.com/lordemusic.

22 "Lorde May Be the New Grammy Favorite, Has Keith Urban Approval," YouTube video, 1:51, posted by "ArtisanNewsService," December 10, 2013, https://www.youtube.com/watch?v=1rkuA_iTJHo.

MORE LORDE INFO

Larson, Lyn. *New Zealand*. Minneapolis: Lerner Publications, 2011.
Learn more about the country Lorde calls home.

Lorde's Facebook Page
https://www.facebook.com/lordemusic
Join more than 4 million fans who like this page.

Lorde's Instagram Page
http://instagram.com/lordemusic
View tons of pics of the stylish songstress.

Lorde's Twitter Page
https://twitter.com/lordemusic
Read Lorde's tweets for up-to-the-minute deets.

Lorde's Website
http://lorde.co.nz
Find links to all of Lorde's social networking sites.

The images in this book are used with the permission of: El Mercurio/Zuma Press/Newscom, pp. 2, 25 (top); AP Photo/Paul A. Hebert/Invision, pp. 3 (top), 14 (bottom left); © Phil Walter/Getty Images, pp. 3 (bottom), 20 (bottom), 22 (top); © Kevin Mazur/WireImage/Getty Images, pp. 4 (bottom left), 5, 9; © Chelsea Laruen/WireImage/Getty Images, p. 4 (right), 21; © Kevin Winter/ WireImage/Getty Images, p. 6 (top); © Lester Cohen/WireImage/Getty Images, p. 6 (bottom); © Jason LaVeris/FilmMagic/Getty Images, p. 7; infusla-276/Chiva/INFphoto.com/Newscom, p. 8 (top); © ScotStock/Alamy, p. 8 (bottom); © James Davies/Alamy, p. 10; © Todd Strand/ Independent Picture Service, p. 11; AP Photo/Matt Sayles/Invision, p. 13; © Christopher Polk/ Getty Images for Coachella, p. 14 (top right); Matt Baron/BEI Images/Rex USA, p. 15; © Victor Chavez/WireImage/Getty Images, p. 16; © Frazer Harrison/Getty Images for Coachella, p. 17; © Al Pereira/WireImage/Getty Images, p. 18; AP Photo/Victoria Will/Invision, p. 19; © Gus Stewart/ WireImage/Getty Images, p. 20 (top); © Groupo13/LatinContent/Getty Images, p. 20 (bottom left); Jim Smeal/BEI Images/Rex USA, p. 20 (bottom right); © Fiona Goodall/Getty Images, p. 23; AGF s.r.l./Rex USA, p. 24; © Dave J. Hogan/Getty Images, p. 25 (bottom); Lucas Jackson/Reuters/ Newscom, p. 26 (bottom); © Frank Hoensch/Redferns/Getty Images, p. 26 (top); © Dimitrios Kambouris/Getty Images for MAC Cosmetics, p. 27; Picture Perfect/Rex USA, p. 28 (left); © Michael Tran/FilmMagic/Getty Images, p. 28 (bottom left); © Ethan Miller/Getty Images, p. 28 (top right); Brian Rasic/Rex USA, p. 29 (bottom left); © Simon James/FilmMagic/Getty Images, p. 29 (right); © Molly Riley/Getty Images, p. 29 (top left).

Front cover: © S_bukley/ImageCollect, (large image); © Tim Mosenflder/WireImage/Getty Images, (inset).

Back cover: © Admedia/ImageCollect.

Main body text set in Shannon Std Book 12/18.
Typeface provided by Monotype Typography.